My Passionate Prayers

My Passionate Prayers

RONKE RUTH ALAO

Copyright © 2013 by Ronke Ruth Alao.

ISBN: Softcover   978-1-4836-8339-3
             Ebook   978-1-4836-8340-9

All rights reserved. No part of this book may be reproduced or transmitted in any form or by any means, electronic or mechanical, including photocopying, recording, or by any information storage and retrieval system, without permission in writing from the copyright owner.

This book was printed in the United States of America.

Rev. date: 08/16/2013

To order additional copies of this book, contact:
Xlibris LLC
0-800-056-3182
www.xlibrispublishing.co.uk
Orders@xlibrispublishing.co.uk

Contents

Foreword..9
Preface..11
Acknowledgements..13
Introduction..15

Prayer list

1. Lead me, Lord..19
2. Let it be to me according to your word...................................21
3. The good hand of God...23
4. God is my Ebenezer..25
5. Lord, bless my hands..27
6. He will ride to my rescue...29
7. Lord, bless my giving..31
8. It is time to advance...33
9. Acquaint yourself with God..35
10. I am blessed...37
11. Prayers from Genesis Chapter 49...39
12. God is my delight..41
13. In God I trust..43
14. My year is blessed...45
15. Touch my lips...47
16. He delivers...49
17. My children shall be taught...51
18. God will establish me...53
19. Gathering to fail..55
20. Every weapon of destruction against me is wasted..............57
21. Let me hear your loving-kindness..59
22. The Lord is my shield..61
23. Make me, Lord...63
24. I am blessed...65

25. Wisdom is of the Lord	67
26. I will flourish in the time of famine	69
27. I will wax great	71
28. I will be fruitful in the land	73
29. I will break forth	75
30. Give me godly virtues	77
31. Step into my boat	79
32. My Lord and shepherd	81
33. Prayers for long life	83
34. Prayer for the children	85
35. Stir up your gift	87
36. Crown me, Lord	89
37. Reward of service	91
38. Designed for purpose	93
39. Thanksgiving	95
40. I will finish well	97
Index	101

Bishop Paul Olukunle Fadeyi
(Grace Outreach Church, London)

My pastor for more than a decade whose passion for prayer and diligence in doing it have taught me the art of prayer and the right way to touch the Father's heart.

Foreword

Pastor Ronke Alao and I both currently serve in the pastoral board of the Grace Outreach Church as ordained pastors under the bishopric of Bishop Paul Fadeyi, the general overseer of the Grace Outreach Church worldwide.

For a long time, I watched Pastor Ronke from afar, fascinated with her gentle personality and drawn to her quiet spirit. As I got to know her and her husband, I confirmed my long-time belief that *inner strength is the virtue of a gentle spirit*.

With this book, Pastor Ronke revealed the secret of that inner strength as the power of her passionate prayers, and the revelation therein is illuminated on every page as you read.

My Passionate Prayers is the best prayer book I have ever read. It is concise and focused on getting you a valuable solution to the problem of ineffective prayer, something that most Christians struggle with.

You see, I believe that praying outside of the will of God is the fundamental reason for ineffective prayers. To pray the will of God, though, requires that you pray the word of God, and that is what this book provides beyond every prayer book you might have read. Pastor Ronke has plunged deep into the well of the word of God and provided you with a path to praying the right prayer over every situation and every problem.

You will turn your prayer life around using this book, not only because it will improve your praying vocabularies, but also because it will drive specificity and target-focused power into your prayers, sending the enemy on the run.

If you invest in the reading and practical utilization of this book, I promise you will have an immeasurable return.

Victor Aigbogun, PhD
Resident Pastor
Grace Outreach Church Riyadh

Preface

Writing this book is, in a way, the fulfilment of a long desire. Most of the prayers in the compilation were done over a period of time and was turned into a book with the specific desire to encourage people, Christians and non-Christians, worldwide not only to pray but also to make prayer an integral part of their existence. Life is full of many challenges, daily activities, and distractions which inevitably force people to re-prioritize life. People now seem to 'major' on the 'minor' and 'minor' on the 'major'. Consequently, people become drained of the essential nutrients that are required to live a fulfilled life on a regular basis.

Here comes the importance of prayer. Indeed, many people, even atheists, often find themselves in situations where they pray, especially after they come to the realization of the limited nature of their strengths, to address a particular situation. However, after their prayers have been answered, they put God back again in the backyard and continue with their lives as usual. This 'mercenary' kind of relationship with God in our prayer life is fundamentally faulty. Prayer should be a way of life rather than a cash-and-carry or a do-on-necessity relationship with God.

A book on prayer is therefore necessary in this regard as prayer is communing with God, the Most High, whose habitation is not in the dwelling of mortals but who has nevertheless made the bodies of those who believe and trust in him his habitation or temple anyway. There is a high sense of awesomeness when consistent prayer communion is made with God, and his presence is considered important and necessary.

I will therefore encourage all to reflect on the scriptural passages which have been quoted and from which the prayers were drawn. Prayer is powerful, and prayers are answered. I can attest to the potency of prayers in my over forty years of existence, and I will encourage people to take them seriously and make them a priority in their daily living. Not just to pray when there is imminent danger, fear, or chaos, but to enjoy a sweet communion of prayer with God at all times, and a beautiful refreshing from the throne of God will always be experienced. Also, great testimony will always abound of deliverance, healing, provision, breakthrough, and advancement when people learn to pray well, effectively, and consistently.

I have not categorized the prayers into any specific groupings. They could be prayed on a forty-day prayer plan. They could also be used during the time of Lent, or any time set apart for fasting and seeking the face of God. On the other hand, it could be used as confessional prayers on a regular basis. Prayer confessions can lift the spirit and ensure good and positive seeds are sown into people's life and future.

Acknowledgements

I offer my sincere appreciation to all my friends, professional colleagues, and loved ones who have, over the years, provided strength and encouragement.

Sincere thanks go to my husband, who has been the oil in the wheel, always encouraging me and patiently listening to every newfound inspirational discovery in the Bible. My children have been sources of enormous delight, especially through generous words of encouragement every step of the way.

Thanks to my parents for all they have done for me. To my siblings and in-laws across the continents, I offer my sincere appreciation.

I am sincerely grateful to all the wonderful people who have taken time to review and provide helpful comments; your contributions and input are greatly valued.

Finally, I must thank the members of Grace Outreach Church for being the 'other family' that is always there. There is really no other place I would rather be on a Sunday morning!

NO OCEAN CAN HOLD IT BACK.

NO RIVER CAN OVERTAKE IT.

NO WHIRLWIND CAN GO FASTER.

NO ARMY CAN DEFEAT IT.

NO LAW CAN STOP IT.

NO DISTANCE CAN SLOW IT.

NO DISEASE CAN CRIPPLE IT.

NO FORCE ON EARTH IS MORE POWERFUL OR EFFECTIVE THAN THE POWER OF PRAYER.

'Prayer, America's Hope', MindyJi

Introduction

I often wonder whether prayer comes under a category of subject that could be taught, or whether the art and act of prayer are things people have to learn in order to be able to pray effectively and achieve results.

My reflection on this point took me to the disciples of Jesus who witnessed him doing many things like teaching, healing, and of course, praying. The one they specifically requested his tutoring on was prayer. This request did not make Jesus feel unhappy; neither did he consider it trivial or unnecessary. Rather, he took it seriously and taught his disciples the now famous the Lord's Prayer.

This led me on a course of wondering why prayer was picked as a subject or an act that required learning. It was then that it occurred to me that Jesus made prayer a lifestyle—praying all night, rising before day to pray, and praying anywhere and anytime. This lifestyle enabled the disciples to realize the centrality of prayers to Jesus' ministry and mission. He also demonstrated the significance of prayer when he alerted his disciples that certain demons can only be cast out by prayer. After his disciples inquired why they could not cast out a particular demon, his response was that conducting such deliverance could only be achieved by prayer and fasting.

It then means that the act or art of prayer can be taught, but the most important thing to understand is that prayer is communion with God. It is a solemn and reverential communication with the unseen yet all-seeing God. Prayer should be a lifestyle for the believer. It should be a practice that is exercised with pleasure and consistency.

It is not practical for someone to commune with themselves in prayer as no result will be achieved. Prayer communion is an effective way to reach the throne room of God. It is the avenue for bringing heaven's attention to the needs of the earth. It is the dynamite for unlocking breakthrough and bringing turnaround in people's lives and situations.

Jesus understood this, practised it, taught it, and lived it. If the son of God could do this, every mortal should not be indifferent to the subject of prayer or to praying as a practical and daily spiritual exercise.

Prayer should therefore be the breath and priority of every believer. Developing a prayer lifestyle is therefore developing a lifestyle that pleases God and a life that will take territories for God's kingdom on earth and will achieve eternal purpose.

Over the years, I have written down my prayers which I prayed during periods of fasting or quiet time before the Lord, and I still pray them regularly. Therefore, as I invite you to accompany me through this journey of my passionate prayers, it is my prayer that you find joy and fulfilment as you develop a consistent prayer life of praying without ceasing. It is also my prayer that as you say the prayers, so it shall be for you in Jesus' name. The Bible says, 'Say unto them, as truly as I live, saith the Lord, as ye have spoken in mine ears, so will I do to you' (Numbers 14:28 KJV). I pray for the affirmation of this in your life.

PRAYER LIST

O thou that hearest prayer, unto thee shall all flesh come.
Psalm 65:2 KJV

The Lord hath heard my supplication; the Lord will receive my prayer.
Psalm 6:9 KJV

The effectual fervent prayer of a righteous man availeth much.
James 5:16 KJV

DAY ONE

MEDITATION

Thus saith the LORD to his anointed, to Cyrus, whose right hand I have holden, to subdue nations before him; and I will loose the loins of kings, to open before him the two leaved gates; and the gates shall not be shut; 2 I will go before thee, and make the crooked places straight: I will break in pieces the gates of brass, and cut in sunder the bars of iron: 3 And I will give thee the treasures of darkness, and hidden riches of secret places, that thou mayest know that I, the LORD, which call thee by thy name, am the God of Israel.

Isaiah 45:1-3 KJV

My confession

The Lord will hold my hands to lead and guide me daily. As he leads me, I will walk with wisdom and insight. I will not walk in error.

Lead me, Lord

- The Lord will hold me by my right hand. He will guide me by his spirit, and I will not walk in darkness.

- As the Lord holds me and leads me through the year, every gate that the enemy has hitherto shut against me will be opened of their own accord and remain open forever.

- The Lord will go before me to remove every barrier to progress and advancement.

- The Lord will create a straight path for me.

- Every crooked path created by the enemy to hinder and slow me down, the Lord will make straight.

- Every gate of bondage, imprisonment, hindrance, limitation, whether made of brass or iron, the Lord will break them into pieces for me and cut them asunder.

- The Lord will give me treasures of darkness, gifts that I did not work for, vineyards that I did not plant, houses that I did not build, lands that I did not purchase.

- The Lord will give me the hidden riches of secret places, divine insight, wisdom, instructions, and skills to operate throughout the year.

- My life will be productive through the blessing of God.

- I will move to another level of grace by his spirit.

- As the blessing of God soaks my life throughout the year, I will be productive for God and advance his kingdom through his grace and gifting.

DAY TWO

MEDITATION

And Samuel grew, and the LORD was with him, and did let none of his words fall to the ground"

1Samuel 3:19 KJV

My confession

As I grow daily in God's presence, I will not be alone; God will enfold me with his everlasting arms. I will be secure in his presence. His promises over my life will not fail.

Let it be to me according to your word

- I will grow physically, spiritually, mentally, and psychologically.

- As the Lord was with Samuel and he grew, I will also grow, and the Lord will be with me day and night.

- May you keep me as the apple of your eyes.

- May your eyes, which are full of light, be upon me daily.

- May your good hand rest upon me for success, prosperity, increase, and blessings.

- May your promises to me not fall to the ground.

- Your promises through your words that you will satisfy me with long life and fulfil my days.

- That wealth will come to me from every nation.

- That I will prosper in health as my soul prospers.

- That I shall be like a tree planted by the side of the rivers of water.

- That I shall bring forth fruits in season.

- That my leaf shall not wither, and whatever I do, I shall prosper.

- That my children shall be taught of the Lord, and great shall be their peace.

- That my latter end shall be better than my beginning.

- None of these promises concerning me shall fall to the ground.

DAY THREE

MEDITATION

Then I told them of the hand of my God which was good upon me; as also the king's words that he had spoken to me. And they said, let us rise up and build so they strengthen their hands for this good work.

Isaiah 45:1-3 KJV

My confession

The good hand of my God will strengthen me to do good. It will help me build waste places. It will help me lift the weak and weary. It will enable me to advance the purpose of God and be a blessing to humanity.

The good hand of God

- May the good hand of the Lord God Almighty be upon me and my family for good.

- May your good hand be upon me for establishment, for growth in the spirit, and for prosperity in health and wealth.

- May your good hand be upon my career, for it to be established and to prosper.

- May your good hand be upon me for victory.

- May your good hand be upon me and my household to prosper and enrich us that no lack or want may be our portion.

- May the good hand of the Lord be upon my larger family for salvation, deliverance, and healing.

- May the good hand of the Lord be upon my friends for fruitfulness and increase.

- May the good hand of the Lord be upon my children for wisdom, understanding, virtue, increase, confidence, boldness, and blessings.

- May the good hand of the Lord be upon them for instruction and godly living all the days of their lives.

- May the good hand of the Lord be upon them for service, anointing, and grace all the days of their lives.

DAY FOUR

MEDITATION

Then Samuel took a stone, and set it between Mizpeh and Shen, and called the name of it Ebenezer, saying, Hitherto hath the LORD helped us.

1 Samuel 7:12 KJV

My confession

The Lord is my help in every situation. In my weakness, I discover his strength. In my sadness, I experience his joy. In my battles, he stays with me to overcome.

God is my Ebenezer

- The Lord is my help and the lifter up of my head.

- My help does not come from the east or west, north or south, but from the Lord who makes the heaven and the earth.

- I will lift up my eyes unto the hills and behold the face of my God for his help.

- Before your face I will find favour.

- I have set my eyes up to you like a flint, and I know that I will not be put to shame.

- In you and through you I receive help for deliverance.

- I receive help for breakthrough, and reproach is removed from my life.

- I receive help for victory, and I'm a winner in the battle of life.

- As the Lord is my help, I am not forsaken.

- As the Lord is my help, I am not forgotten.

- As the Lord is my help, I walk in triumph.

- As the Lord is my help, I have no reason to fear.

- The Lord is my help in every situation both now and in the future.

- He is my Ebenezer.

DAY FIVE

MEDITATION

Let his hands be sufficient for him.

Deuteronomy 33:7 KJV

My confession

This hand will be sufficient for my needs.
Empower my hand to be productive.
Let this hand be anointed to be fruitful.
Let my hand reap the labours of its hard work.

Lord, bless my hands

- Lord, let my hands be sufficient for me in life.
- Bless my hands with the blessings you alone can give.
- Enrich my hands with the dew of heaven.
- Let my hands be fruitful and productive.
- Whatever I lay my hands on, do let it prosper and yield great gains.
- Whatever I touch with my hands, let it multiply and yield increase.
- Whomever I lay my hands on to bless, let them be blessed indeed.
- Let the touch of my hand bring comfort.
- Let the touch of my hand be an extension of God's hand for strength to the weak.
- Let the touch of my hand bring encouragement to the weary.
- Let the touch of my hand cause faith to arise in the heart of the faint-hearted.
- Let the touch of my hand bring healing to a broken body.
- Let my hands be anointed perpetually with the oil of God.
- Let my hands bring me great wealth and riches.

DAY SIX

MEDITATION

Who rideth upon the heaven in thy help and in His Excellency on the sky.

Deuteronomy 33:26 KJV

My confession

The Lord will locate me in every situation. He will ride to my rescue and salvation. He will ride to deliver me from vicissitudes of life. He will ride to secure me from harm.

He will ride to my rescue

- The Lord will ride upon the heaven to help me.

- You are my help continually and the lifter up of my head.

- You will stretch forth your hands to deliver me from falling.

- You will pull me out of miry clay and set my feet on the rock to stay.

- You will draw me from the pit of ignorance to a bright and shining light of your wondrous knowledge.

- You will give your angels charge over me to bear me on their wings.

- Your help over my life is as sure as the daylight.

- You are my present help in distress.

- You hear and answer my call morning, day, and night.

- You will rescue me from every attack of the enemy.

- I receive heavenly help on earth.

- You will ride in your majesty and splendour to embrace me and comfort me on every side.

DAY SEVEN

MEDITATION

Now he that ministereth seed to the sower both minister bread for your food, and multiply your seed sown, and increase the fruits of your righteousness; Being enriched in everything to all bountifulness, which causeth through us thanksgiving to God.

2 Corinthians 9:10-11 KJV

My confession

My giving will be received.
I will receive bountifully as I give.
My giving will not be rejected.
My giving will attract blessings and increase to my life.
As I give, I will never be in want.

Lord, bless my giving

- Lord, seed does not exist in a vacuum; you are the provider of seed. Bless me with seed so that I can be a good sower.

- Lord, let my seed never run out.

- Let my seed be plenteous and be sufficient for food and planting.

- Lord, you provided manna to the Israelites in the wilderness, and it was food for them daily. Let me also receive your daily manna so that there will always be food in my house.

- Lord Jesus, you are the bread of heaven. As you satisfy my spiritual hunger, let my physical, financial, and career hunger be satisfied.

- Let me never experience physical or spiritual malnutrition.

- Lord, divinely multiply my seed sown to a thousandfold, for you are the God of increase; let your increase be upon my seed.

- Lord, increase the fruit of my righteousness, and let the fruit of righteousness be evident in my life.

- Let situations or circumstances not affect my right standing with you; rather, let me live to please you daily.

- Riches and wealth come from you; let me be enriched in everything to all bountifulness.

- Let my life be enriched with prosperity in my health, body, and soul.

- Let my life be enriched with gold and silver.

- Let my life be enriched with the joy of the Lord.

DAY EIGHT

MEDITATION

And the LORD spake unto me, saying, Ye have compassed this mountain long enough: turn you northward.

Deuteronomy 2:2-3 KJV

My confession

I will not be a rolling stone that gathers no moss.
I will not roam aimlessly in life.
I will aim at the target with precision.
I will advance in life and will not stop until I reach the promised land and a place of destiny.

It is time to advance

- Lord, I break free from every stagnancy in my life.
- I declare that I advance in life.
- I declare that my career and business flourish.
- I declare that my spiritual life is fruitful.
- Every mountain of limitation is removed from my life.
- I speak progress and fruitfulness into everything I set my hands to do.
- Henceforth, I advance to fulfil my destiny.
- I advance to prosper.
- I advance to the promised land, and I declare victory in my journey.
- The Israelites declared in Deuteronomy 2:36, 'There was not one city too strong for us: the Lord our God delivered all unto us.'
- As I advance in life, no stronghold will be too strong for me to overcome or conquer.
- I have victory over every obstacle created to hinder my progress.
- I have deliverance over every lack or limitation on my way.
- I declare abundance, prosperity, and victory as I attain the land of promise.

DAY NINE

MEDITATION

Acquaint now thyself with him, and be at peace: thereby good shall come unto thee.

Job 22:21 KJV

My confession

My heart draws close to God. I soak and bask myself in the bath of his pleasure. I daily revere and rejoice in his presence. I will daily behold his glory until I see him face-to-face.

Acquaint yourself with God

- Lord, I will acquaint myself with you.

- As I acquaint myself with you, Lord, I shall be at peace.

- Good shall come to me.

- The wealth of the nations shall be mine.

- I shall be built up, and I will wax strong in the spirit.

- I will put iniquity far away from my life,

- I will lay up good treasures and will not be like the prodigal son.

- Lord, you shall be my refuge, fortress, and defence.

- I will have plenty of silver and gold.

- My delight shall be in you, the Almighty God.

- As I pray to you, I will be heard.

- I will live to pay my vows.

- I will decree a thing, and it shall be established.

- The light of God shall shine upon my ways.

- When people are cast down, discouraged, and weary, I will lift them up.

- As I acquaint myself with you, like Father Abraham, I will be called a friend of God.

DAY TEN

MEDITATION

For the LORD thy God hath blessed thee in all the works of thy hand: he knoweth thy walking through this great wilderness: these forty years the LORD thy God hath been with thee; thou hast lacked nothing.

Deuteronomy 2:7 KJV

My confession

The work of my hand is fruitful.
The work of my hand is creative.
The work of my hand is blessed.
The work of my hand is excellent.
The work of my hand will yield great gain.

I am blessed

- As the Lord blessed the Israelites in all the works of their hands, I declare that all the works of my hands are blessed.

- I declare that I am blessed to flourish.

- God guided the walking of the Israelites through the wilderness; he will guide me as I walk through this life, and I will not walk alone.

- I will walk with purpose, and my steps will be ordered by God.

- The Israelites lacked nothing good throughout their forty years' walk in the wilderness. I declare that I will lack nothing good as I walk through life.

- I will not lack for joy of the Lord.

- My head will not lack for oil.

- My hands will not lack for money.

- My mind will not lack for fruitful and path-breaking ideas.

- I declare that I will not lack for success in my career and business.

- I will not lack for good health.

- The gift and love of God will not be lacking in my life.

DAY ELEVEN

MEDITATION

All these are the twelve tribes of Israel: and this is it that their father spake unto them, and blessed them; every one according to his blessing he blessed them.

Genesis 49:28 KJV

My confession

The hand of God is upon me to bless and lift me up.
By reason of God's blessings, I will walk in the supernatural.
I will make giant strides in life. I will attain great heights.

Prayers from Genesis Chapter 49

- I will excel and have pre-eminence in life.

- I will be stable in mind, thoughts, and emotion.

- I will experience stability in every area of my life—family, career, business, and finances.

- God will be the stability of my life.

- I will live a life that is worthy of praise, honour, and recognition.

- May my hand be on the neck of my enemies.

- No enemy will prevail or rejoice over me.

- No enemy of sickness, defeat, lack, intimidation, or oppression will have upper hand in my life.

- I will be a fruitful bough, a fruitful bough by a well, whose branches run over the wall.

- May the arms of my hands be made strong and active by the hands of the Mighty God, the Great Shepherd, the Rock of my salvation.

- May the Almighty God bless me with the blessings of the heavens above, blessings lying in the deep beneath, blessing of the breasts and of the womb.

- May the blessings of God on me be as lasting as the bounties of the eternal hills.

DAY TWELVE

MEDITATION

Delight thyself also in the LORD: and he shall give thee the desires of thine heart.

Psalm 37:4 KJV

My confession

God is my delight, and he delights in me. As the apple of his eyes, I am tattooed on the palm of his hands, and he delights in me. He delights in me to bless my life with the desires of my heart.

God is my delight

- I will desire God in my desires.

- My desires will align with God's desires for my life.

- I will live to please God and honour him with my life.

- This year, all my desires in accordance with the will and purpose of God will be fulfilled.

- I will not have lustful desires.

- I will not desire abominable things.

- I will not desire the forbidden fruit of sin.

- I will not desire the onion and garlic of Egypt to return to bondage but will be satisfied with the milk and honey of the promised land and will live in liberty.

- I will not desire gold and silver at the expense of people's lives.

- I will not desire things that do not profit.

- I will not desire things that will bring stagnation to my spiritual life.

- I will not desire things that will be destructive to my body and soul.

- Every ungodly desire from the pit of hell is crushed.

- I desire God's desire, and my desires are fulfilled in Jesus' name.

DAY THIRTEEN

MEDITATION

Blessed is the man that trusteth in the LORD, and whose hope the LORD is.

Jeremiah 17:7 KJV

My confession

My trust is in the Lord. He is my hope and confidence. I rely on him daily as a rock and sure refuge.

In God I trust

- Lord, I trust you as my life and the length of my days.

- I trust you as my help.

- I trust you as my source and provider.

- I trust you as the lifter up of my head.

- I trust you as my confidence.

- I trust you as my glory.

- I trust you as the health of my flesh.

- I trust you as my keeper and strong tower.

- I trust you as my banner and strong refuge.

- I trust you as my exceeding great reward.

- I trust you as my hope.

- In the morning, afternoon, and night you are my hope of glory.

- You are my hope of joy.

- You are my hope of blessings and good things.

- Lord, I know that as I trust and hope in you, I will be like a tree that is planted by the waters.

- I will flourish on every side.

- I will not see when heat comes.

DAY FOURTEEN

MEDITATION

Thou crownest the year with thy goodness; and thy paths drop fatness.

Psalm 23:6 KJV

My confession

My year is blessed.
My year is crowned with God's goodness.
My year is full of pleasant things.
My year will be filled with God's glory.

My year is blessed

- The Lord will crown the year and beyond with his goodness in my life, home, and family.

- The Lord will cause me to experience favour, uplifting, advancement, and progress in my spiritual, physical, career, and financial life.

- The path of the Lord drops fatness. I will walk in the fatness of the Lord.

- I will not experience dryness in any area of my life.

- Drought will not be my portion.

- I will be fruitful in and out of season.

- My leaves will not fall prematurely.

- I will not age or die before my time.

- My barn will be filled with plenty of good fruits, and I shall provide a shade.

- My life will be a blessing to many.

- My year is enriched with God's divine presence.

- I will be guarded and directed throughout the year by the Holy Spirit.

- I will walk in divine counsel throughout the year.

- I will operate in the wisdom of God throughout the year.

- My life will manifest the fullness of God's glory and power.

DAY FIFTEEN

MEDITATION

And he laid it upon my mouth, and said, Lo, this hath touched thy lips; and thine iniquity is taken away, and thy sin purged.

Isaiah 6:7 KJV

My confession

My lips are cleansed and sanctified.
My lips are purified by God.
My lips will utter words of life.
My lips will speak words of healing and comfort.

Touch my lips

- Lord, touch my lips with your wholesome hand.

- Lord, let every sin and iniquity that my lips have spoken be forgiven.

- Let my lips be purified to speak the word of life and truth.

- Let my lips be a spring of life through the wholesome words of God that will flow freely from it.

- Let my lips be a channel to bless and not curse.

- Let my lips honour God all the days of my life.

- Let no words of death ever proceed out of my lips.

- Let no words of defeat, discouragement, or negativity proceed from my lips.

- Let the words of strength and faith freely flow through my lips.

- Words that build up, words that advance, words that encourage, words that save and heal, let them flow ceaseless from my mouth.

- My lips will not be employed by the devil but will be totally surrendered to God.

- My words, through my lips, will be a spring of life to all around me.

DAY SIXTEEN

MEDITATION

Who delivered us from so great a death, and doth deliver: in whom we trust that he will yet deliver us.

2 Corinthians 1:10 KJV

My confession

You deliver me always.
You are my great deliverer.
I will not fall like a prey.
I will not be a victim in life.
God will deliver me from every evil and the imagination of the enemy.
I will be delivered continually.

He delivers

- God is my great deliverer.

- He delivers me from sudden death, sickness, and disease, from poverty and lack, from the scheming and devices of the evil one.

- He delivers me from the arrows that fly by day and the pestilence that waste at noonday.

- He preserves my life and sustains me by his spirit; hence, I live each day breathing through him because in him I live, move, and have my being.

- He delivered me over the years, and he's still delivering me, and he will yet deliver me.

- Lord, I'm grateful for your great deliverance.

- For the deliverance from physical, spiritual, and financial death.

- You did not allow the enemy to rejoice over me, but you have saved me from his devices.

- Every hole the enemy dug for my burial, you covered and erased.

- Thank you because on a daily basis you are still delivering me through the precious blood of the Lord Jesus Christ.

- By reason of your great deliverance, I will continue to be alive in you.

DAY SEVENTEEN

MEDITATION

And all thy children shall be taught of the LORD; and great shall be the peace of thy children.

Isaiah 54:13 KJV

My confession

You are my instructor.
You taught me from my youth.
You taught me to know and to love you.
I will continue to learn at your feet.
Your teaching will advance me and enable me to grow in spiritual strength and stamina.
Your teaching will enable me to grow in wisdom.

My children shall be taught

- My children shall be taught of the Lord.
- They shall be instructed by the Holy Spirit.
- They will hear the voice and instructions of God, and their ears will be blocked to the voice and instructions of strangers.
- They will not be instructed or influenced by the world or the media.
- As they are instructed of the Lord, they will grow in wisdom, knowledge, and understanding.
- They will have divine insight beyond their years.
- They will operate in the wisdom of God.
- They will make right decisions and choices in life through the help of the Holy Spirit.
- Throughout the year and beyond, my children shall have peace, and they will walk in the path of peace.
- There will be no unrest in their lives, health, or academic work.
- They will not cause me grief, and they will not cause God grief.
- They will not cause me sorrow, and I will not be sorrowed over their lives.
- They will not be defiled.
- They will live purposeful lives.
- They will identify their gifting early in life.
- They will use their gifts profitably to advance the purpose of God, and their gift will bless humanity.
- They will live fulfilled lives.

DAY EIGHTEEN

MEDITATION

In righteousness shalt thou be established: thou shalt be far from oppression; for thou shalt not fear: and from terror; for it shall not come near thee.

Isaiah 54:14 KJV

My confession

I am established in God.
I am established in life.
No gathering will destabilize me.
No attack against me will work.
I am fortified by God's divine protection.

God will establish me

- God will divinely establish me in his purpose and counsel.

- My foundation is sure on the Lord Jesus Christ, and no counsel from the pit of hell will shift me from my solid foundation.

- As I am divinely established, oppression will be far from my life, whether physical or spiritual.

- I will continue to walk in the liberty with which Christ has made me free.

- I will not be afraid neither will I live in fear, for God has not given me the spirit of fear but of love and sound mind.

- No terror will come near me as I travel to work and back.

- No terror will come near me in the bus or train.

- No terror will come near me as I travel in the air.

- No terror at my place of abode.

- I am protected from every wiles of the evil one.

- The hedges of God's fire are around me.

- I am secured under the strong tower of the Lord's name.

- The blood of Jesus is my shield and covering.

- By the grace of God, I will dwell in safety.

DAY NINETEEN

MEDITATION

Behold, they shall surely gather together, but not by me: whosoever shall gather together against thee shall fall for thy sake.

Isaiah 54:15 KJV

My confession

The gathering of evil against me will not prosper.
The gathering of the enemy against me will turn to confusion.
Every gathering against the plans, purpose, and counsel of God for my life will fail. It will not see the light of day.

Gathering to fail

- Every gathering, device, and purpose of evil against me will not stand.

- As they gather against me, they will fall for my sake.

- No gathering against the purpose of God for my life will see the light of day.

- As a child of God, my heritage is victory, and I am victorious continually.

- No divination or enchantment against my life will stand.

- I am a terror to the kingdom of darkness.

- I speak confusion to every gathering against my life.

- I declare that the gathering of the enemy against me scatters.

- Every curse pronounced against my life or destiny is null and void.

- No encampment against my life, health, finances, ministry, and family will succeed.

- Only the angels of the Lord encamp around me, and they deliver me from every attack of the enemy.

- I am secured and preserved by God's power.

DAY TWENTY

MEDITATION

No weapon that is formed against thee shall prosper; and every tongue that shall rise against thee in judgment thou shalt condemn. This is the heritage of the servants of the LORD, and their righteousness is of me, saith the LORD.

Isaiah 54:17 KJV

My confession

I am an instrument and a weapon of goodwill in God's hands.
No weapon of destruction will work against me.
No utterance of evil or divination will overcome me.
I am an overcomer, and I have victory over evil orchestrated against my life.
I have victory through the blood of Jesus continually. I am, daily, victorious.

w

Every weapon of destruction against me is wasted

- I am an instrument in the hand of God, his workmanship created to advance his purpose on earth.

- Therefore, no weapon fashioned against my life by any man or spirit will prosper.

- I am totally yielded to the Lord.

- Like clay in the potter's hand, I surrender myself to be moulded and fashioned for my life's assignment.

- I will execute every assignment with precision and accuracy as I am led by the Spirit.

- The waster will be far from my life.

- The waster will not destroy the work of my hands.

- Every tongue of curse against my life will turn to blessings.

- Every tongue of condemnation against my life will turn to praise.

- Every false tongue of accusation against me is condemned.

- Every false tongue against my testimony is silenced.

- I prevail over every weapon of the enemy and the tongue of the wicked.

DAY TWENTY ONE

MEDITATION

Cause me to hear thy loving kindness in the morning; for in thee do I trust: cause me to know the way wherein I should walk; for I lift up my soul unto thee.

Psalm 143:8 KJV

My confession

My ears are anointed to hear your voice.
To hear your words of love and instruction.
Your words will guide me daily to walk in the path of truth, holiness, and integrity.

Let me hear your loving-kindness

- Lord, I will hear your loving-kindness all day long.
- I will not hear hate or death.
- I will not hear poverty, lack, or disease.
- As you speak to me daily, I will continue to trust in you.
- You are my confidence and my exceeding great reward.
- You are my buckler and my shield.
- You are my solid rock upon which I lean and upon which my life anchors.
- As I trust in you, I will know which way to walk.
- In my spiritual life, daily life, career, and family, I will not walk in error.
- As I listen and hear you speak to me, I will walk in the wisdom and fear of God.
- I will hear your words of instruction with clarity.
- When I hear you, I will respond.
- I will take heed to your words of loving-kindness.
- I will cause your loving-kindness to take root in my heart.

DAY TWENTY TWO

MEDITATION

For the LORD God is a sun and shield: the LORD will give grace and glory: no good thing will he withhold from them that walk uprightly.

Psalm 84:11 KJV

My confession

You are my covering, O Lord.
I am shielded under your banner.
Under your covering, you meet all my needs.
You satisfy my life with good things.

The Lord is my shield

- The Lord is a shield and covering for all those who put their trust in him.

- Just as it is impossible to draw near the sun and live, everything and anything that draws near me to cause harm or affliction will be burnt to ashes.

- The shield of God is impenetrable; hence, no arrow of the enemy can penetrate the shield of God to touch my life.

- The shield of his everlasting arms covers me.

- I am protected in his care and presence.

- God is a giver of good things, including grace and glory. I receive the fullness of his grace and glory into my life.

- I walk gracefully, and my comportment is in grace.

- His glory is evident in every area of my life.

- I will walk uprightly before him all the days of my life.

- My garment of purity will not be tainted with sin.

- No good thing will be held back from my life.

- I will continue to walk steadfastly in truth and faith before him.

DAY TWENTY THREE

MEDITATION

And he saith unto them, Follow me, and I will make you . . .

Matthew 4:19 KJV

My confession

Only a Creator can make.
You are the Creator of the universe, and you created me in your image.
You will make me, Lord.
You will fashion me.
You will mould me as a worthy instrument in your hand.

Make me, Lord

- You alone can make a man or woman, and when you make, no man can break.

- The making of God will make me wholesome.

- The making of God will transform my life.

- The making of God will cause his purpose to be fulfilled in my life.

- The making of God will cause me to be fulfilled.

- The making of God will mark me out.

- The making of God will make me productive and fruitful.

- The making of God will put his stamp of approval on my life.

- The making of God will cause me to make it in life.

- The making of God will advertise me.

- The making of God will cause me to be made for life.

- Lord, make me, fashion me, mould me, and let me be all that you want me to be as I follow you in faith and holiness.

DAY TWENTY FOUR

MEDITATION

Blessed be the God and Father of our Lord Jesus Christ, who hath blessed us with all spiritual blessings in heavenly places in Christ.

Ephesians 1:3 KJV

My confession

I receive God's spiritual blessings into my life.
My life is complete and whole with God's blessings.
I am indeed a delightsome child, and every eye that sees me will acknowledge that I am a blessed child of the living God.

I am blessed

- I am blessed and not cursed.

- Spiritual blessings imply wholeness of body, spirit, and soul. I am blessed in all entirety.

- I am blessed in whatever I lay my hands on to do.

- I am blessed in my home, in my coming in and in my going out.

- I am blessed in my career and business.

- The blessing of the Lord will advertise me and give me recognition.

- The blessing of the Lord will reveal his glory in me.

- The blessing of God makes me rich, and it adds no sorrow with it.

- The blessing of the Lord makes me productive and fruitful.

- The blessing of the Lord will enable me to attract favour from unusual sources.

- The blessings of the Lord will attract to my life helpers of destiny.

- The blessing of the Lord will make me soar like the eagles.

- The blessing of the Lord propels me to great altitude in my walk of faith.

- By reason of God's blessings, my life will be profitable.

- By reason of God's blessings, everything I lay my hands on to do will blossom and flourish.

- As I am blessed spiritually, everything physical around me reveals the blessings of the Lord.

DAY TWENTY FIVE

MEDITATION

For the LORD giveth wisdom: out of his mouth cometh knowledge and understanding. He layeth up sound wisdom for the righteous: he is a buckler to them that walk uprightly.

Proverbs 2:6-7 KJV

My confession

The wisdom of God is upon me to live a fulfilled life.
I will think and speak with wisdom.
I will manage the affairs of my life with wisdom and discretion.
Wisdom and knowledge will work for me, with me, and through me.

Wisdom is of the Lord

- Lord, fill my heart with your wisdom.

- Let my wisdom surpass that of Solomon because your word says that the glory of the latter house will surpass that of the former.

- Let the sound wisdom that you have laid in store for the righteous be my portion.

- Lord, let my heart be filled with knowledge and understanding needed to operate at a time such as this.

- Help me to think and speak at a level beyond my years.

- I declare that I have sound wisdom to operate in my ministry, career, and finances.

- Let wisdom manifest in my life as I relate with people.

- Let your wisdom in my heart confound the adversary of my life.

- Let your wisdom in my life advance me.

- Let your wisdom advertise me as it advertised Solomon.

- Let your wisdom reveal divine excellence in and through me.

- Let my destiny shine by the reason of God's wisdom upon my life.

- Like the Psalmist declared, so I declare that I will speak of wisdom and the meditation of my heart shall be of understanding always.

- Let your wisdom operate in my life without measure.

DAY TWENTY SIX

MEDITATION

And there was a famine in the land, beside the first famine that was in the days of Abraham . . . Then Isaac sowed in that land, and received in the same year a hundredfold: and the LORD blessed him.

Genesis 26:1a, 12 KJV

My confession

My life will not experience famine.
I will flourish continually.
My life will be fruitful.
My land will yield a hundredfold increase even in time of famine.

I will flourish in the time of famine

- Lord, I recognize you as the Lord of the harvest.

- I acknowledge you as the only one who can bring yield and multiplication to anything sown.

- Lord, as I sow, let me reap a bountiful harvest.

- There are categories of harvest—thirty, sixty, and hundredfold. Let my harvest be hundredfold.

- Let my harvest fill the barn of my life to satisfy my needs and also enable me to be a blessing.

- Lord, as I sow in tears, I pray that I will reap in joy.

- Lord, you have said in your word that those who serve you will not serve you in vain. Therefore, Lord, let me reap a harvest of service.

- As I sow my life in your vineyard, serving you with diligence, I will reap a harvest of abundant and eternal life.

- As I sow in faithfulness and love to advance your purpose and kingdom on earth, it will translate to eternal rewards for me and my descendants.

- As I sow my time, talent, and treasure, you will cause me to reap a harvest of blessings and fulfilment.

- Let my harvest of service lead to divine uplifting, financial prosperity, long life, advancement in my career, favour on every side, and abundance in my life and family.

DAY TWENTY SEVEN

MEDITATION

And the man waxed great, and went forward, and grew until he became very great.

Genesis 26:13 KJV

My confession

The Lord is with me; therefore, I will wax great.
I will not wax small.
I will not be insignificant.
I will be relevant in my career, business, and community.
I will matter where it matters, and I will be reckoned with.

I will wax great

- As a descendant of Isaac by the spirit, the blessing of Abraham upon Isaac is mine.

- I declare in the name of Jesus that I will wax great.

- I declare that I will go forwards and never backwards.

- I declare that I will advance and never retreat.

- I confess and declare that my coast is enlarged, my horizon is broadened, and my sphere of influence is widened.

- I declare that I will grow and become very great in whatever I lay my hand on to do.

- I will be lifted from a level of obscurity to prominence.

- I will not be anonymous in this life.

- Every limitation over my life is removed.

- I will wax great in my faith.

- I will wax great into spiritual maturity.

- I will grow very great in the work of God, in my ministry, in my career, and in my service to humanity.

- I will wax great in my love for God, my Bible study life, and my prayer life.

DAY TWENTY EIGHT

MEDITATION

And he removed from thence, and digged another well; and for that they strove not: and he called the name of it Rehoboth; and he said, For now the LORD hath made room for us, and we shall be fruitful in the land.

Genesis 26:22 KJV

My confession

The Lord has made room for me in this life.
I cease from every struggle.
Therefore, I have peace and rest.
The work of my hand is productive, and prosperity encompasses my life.

I will be fruitful in the land

- This is the land that the Lord has planted me in, and he has made room for me.

- In this land, God has blessed me with goods and good spiritual heritage.

- I pray that I will continue to be fruitful in the land.

- I will continue to be productive.

- I will continue to excel and do well.

- I will be favoured in the land.

- As Joseph thrived and flourished greatly in the land of Egypt, a foreign land, so will I thrive and flourish greatly in this land.

- God will fill my life with the milk and honey of this land.

- I will not be a victim in this land.

- I will not live in debt in this land.

- I will not be oppressed in the land.

- The key to unlock the wealth of this land will be released.

- This land will work for me, and it will add to me.

- I will also be an added value to this land.

DAY TWENTY NINE

MEDITATION

And it came to pass, as he drew back his hand, that, behold, his brother came out: and she said, How hast thou broken forth?

Genesis 38:29 KJV

My confession

I will not be held back in life.
Nothing will slow me down from moving forward.
I will break forth from every obstacle and hindrance.
I will not be pushed to the back.
I will break forth even from behind to destiny.

I will break forth

- I will break forth in Jesus' name.

- I will break forth from obscurity to prominence in this life.

- I will break forth like the light of the day and the morning sun.

- I will break forth with the favour of God.

- I will break forth with the blessing of God.

- I will break forth from poverty and lack to prosperity and abundance.

- I will break forth to excellent health in body and total well-being.

- I will break forth to excellence in life.

- I will break forth to advancement in this life.

- I will break forth to promotion, career, and business success.

- I will break forth to increase.

- I will break forth to stability and grace.

- I shall not draw back to failure, stagnancy, servitude, poverty, and lack.

- I will not draw back to sin, unrighteousness, and iniquity.

- I will not draw back from being a blessing.

- I will break forth to the praise and glory of the Almighty God.

DAY THIRTY

MEDITATION

And beside this, giving all diligence, add to your faith virtue; and to virtue knowledge;6 And to knowledge temperance; and to temperance patience; and to patience godliness;7 And to godliness brotherly kindness; and to brotherly kindness charity.8 For if these things be in you, and abound, they make you that ye shall neither be barren nor unfruitful in the knowledge of our Lord Jesus Christ.

2 Peter 1:5-8 KJV

My confession

My life is filled with God's virtue.
I am a virtuous child of God.
I am a child with God's excellent spirit.
I operate by the help of the Holy Spirit; therefore, godly virtues are evident in my life.

Give me godly virtues

- Lord, help me to grow in faith daily.
- Help me not to be easily moved or shaken by circumstances; rather, let the root of my faith in you be deep and enduring.
- Let me be strengthened spiritually and physically as I grow in faith.
- Lord, let your virtue be seen in me.
- Let me not just be a virtuous woman to the world, but let me be a woman of virtue to you and my family.
- Lord, fill my heart with your knowledge.
- Give me understanding of the times I am in, and give me knowledge of the things to come.
- Lord, help me to have good temperance and to live at peace with all men.
- Let me not exhibit sudden or uncontrollable anger.
- Remove any form of quarrelsome spirit from my life.
- Remove every form of moodiness from my heart.
- Let my life radiate cheerfulness and joy continually.
- Lord, help me to exhibit godliness through the way I talk and relate with people.
- Let me be seen and known to be godlike in my attitude and way of life.
- Lord, help me to exhibit patience when I should.
- Help me not to be hasty to my hurt or someone else's hurt.
- Help me to patiently wait upon you until my chance comes.
- Let my heart never be weary as I patiently trust you for uplifting, breakthrough, and blessing on my life and family.
- Lord, help me to show brotherly kindness at all times.
- Help me to be my brother and sister's keeper and not killer.
- Let me show sympathy, empathy, and compassion when they are needed.
- Let love flow in my heart towards others.
- Lord, help me show and practise charity, for in giving we receive and in sowing we reap.
- Let the love, care, kindness, and giving that I sow in other lives return to me as good harvest in a hundredfold.

DAY THIRTY ONE

MEDITATION

And he saw them toiling in rowing; for the wind was contrary unto them: and about the fourth watch of the night he cometh unto them, walking upon the sea, and would have passed by them.

Mark 6:48 KJV

My confession

The Lord will not pass me by.
I keep my focus on him continually.
He will step into my situation and life.
He will bring ease and calm into every turbulence.
He will satisfy me with the abundant peace of his presence.

Step into my boat

- Lord, how I have struggled in my strength. I thought I could help myself, but now I know that my help comes from you, the maker of heaven and earth.

- Lord, please do not pass me by, but rather step into my boat and let me experience your calm and peace.

- Lord, don't look at me from afar as I struggle, for my strength is spent.

- Lord, let every hard toiling in my life cease.

- Let things come to me more easily.

- Let me achieve greater altitude without struggle.

- Let me progress in life without toil.

- Lord, step into my boat and give me victory over everything that seems contrary.

- Lord, let the struggle in my life cease; let it be over, and let me walk and operate in the victory of the Lord Jesus.

- As Jesus steps into the boat of my finances, I have abundance, prosperity, and more than enough.

- As the Lord steps into my boat, the raging waves of debt, poverty, and lack disappear.

- As the Lord steps into the boat of my career, I progress, I soar like the eagles, and I receive elevation.

- As Jesus Christ steps into the boat of my marriage and home, there is flourishing, love, tenderness, and harmony.

- As the Lord Jesus steps into my larger family, there is salvation, deliverance, and establishment.

DAY THIRTY TWO

MEDITATION

The LORD is my shepherd; I shall not want.

Psalm 23:1 KJV

My confession

You are the Good Shepherd of my life.
I will not be confused, and I will not walk in dry places.
You will shepherd my life to the place of green pastures.
You will direct my path to a place of safety and provision daily.

My Lord and shepherd

- Lord, you are my shepherd, the shepherd of my soul and life.

- As the shepherd attends to the sheep, so you also attend to my every care and need.

- As the shepherd watches over the sheep, so you watch over me day and night.

- You do not sleep in the midnight hours, and you are never weary during the day as you attend to my needs.

- As the shepherd protects the sheep from all manners of danger, so you protect me, Lord.

- You protect me from the arrows that fly by day and the pestilence that waste at noonday.

- Your watchful eyes are upon me continually.

- As the shepherd guides the sheep from straying, so you guide me in all my ways.

- As the shepherd leads the sheep to green pastures where there is food and water, so you lead me to a place of provision, abundance, and prosperity.

- You lead me to the meadow and a fountain of living water so I can eat and drink and be satisfied.

- As the sheep hears the voice of the shepherd, so I hear the voice of the Lord, and my ears are blocked to the voice of strangers.

- My shepherd, my keeper, to you alone I look for security, provision, and salvation.

DAY THIRTY THREE

MEDITATION

O My God, take me not away in the midst of my days; thy years are throughout all generations.

Psalm 102:24 KJV

My confession

I have the abundant life of God to fulfil my purpose and destiny.
I will not exit before my time.
I will live to complete my assignment.
With long life, he will satisfy me, and he will show me his salvation.

Prayers for long life

- Lord, take me not away in the midst of my days.
- Take me not away before my due time.
- Lord, satisfy me with long life.
- Let my days be fulfilled.
- Prolong my life to see good years ahead.
- Let me not die but live to declare your glory in the land of the living.
- Let me live to see the good of my children and their children.
- Let the years ahead be the best years of my life.
- Let my latter end be better than my beginning.
- Let every potential that you have given me be maximized on this earth.
- In due time, let me come back home emptied of all the gifting you've given me because they've been used.
- Lord, let me not suffer affliction.
- Let no plague come near my dwelling place.
- Both now and in the years ahead, let me continue to enjoy soundness of body and mind.
- Lord, keep my mind steady and alert.
- Let my memory not depreciate.
- Let my bones not grow weak.
- Let my hands and knees not grow feeble.
- Let my eyes not grow dim.
- Let my face not be wrinkled.
- Strengthen my heart each day to love you and proclaim your highest praise.
- Let me not become slow of speech.
- Let my voice be continually clear to declare your love, goodness, faithfulness, and favour.
- Let my ears be anointed at all times to hear your voice.
- Let my entire life be full of your light continually.
- The Bible says that Job lived to old age and was full of days, Lord; let that be my portion in this life.

DAY THIRTY FOUR

MEDITATION

That our sons may be as plants grown up in their youth; that our daughters may be as corner stones, polished after the similitude of a palace.

Psalm 144:12 KJV

My confession

My children will grow and flourish.
They will wax great in life and excel.
They will live to fulfil purpose.
They will accomplish great things for God and humanity.
Their lives will be fruitful and productive.
They will impact their generation positively.
Whatever they lay their hands on to do will prosper.

Prayer for the children

- Lord, make my children excel and have pre-eminence in life.
- You are the stability of their lives, Lord. Make them stable in mind, thoughts, and emotions and in every area of their lives.
- Lord, let them live a life that is worthy of praise, honour, and recognition.
- Let no enemy prevail over their lives.
- Let them be like a fruitful tree beside a fountain, and their branches a shade over the wall.
- Let the arms of their hands be made strong and active by the hands of the mighty God.
- Let your blessings upon their lives be as lasting as the bounties of the eternal hills.
- Let them be of graceful beauty like the pillars of a palace wall.
- Lord, let them have reverential fear of God.
- Satisfy them with long life, and show them your salvation.
- Let affliction be far from their lives, and let their lives not be plagued by illness, sickness, or disease.
- Lord, let their lives be marked with success, and let them be celebrated in life.
- Lord, make them fruitful in life and productive in the work of their hands.
- Let them not experience delay in life.
- Lord, let them not be defiled.
- Keep them as the apple of your eyes, and let them live to serve you.
- At the appointed time, Lord, bless them with a good and happy home.

DAY THIRTY FIVE

MEDITATION

Wherefore I put thee in remembrance that thou stir up the gift of God, which is in thee by the putting on of my hands.

2 Timothy 1:6 KJV

My confession

My gift will make room for me.
My gift will profit my life.
My gift will bring me prominence.
My gift will be profitable to advance the kingdom of God and his purpose on earth, and it will benefit humanity.

Stir up your gift

- Lord, I thank you for your gifts in my life.
- I appreciate and recognize that you have blessed me with gifts.
- Lord, give me the grace to maximize my gifts.
- Give me avenues and opportunities for the expression of these gifts.
- Let my gifts not be dormant.
- Help me to be fruitful and productive for you as I exercise my gifts.
- Let my gifts make room for me.
- Through my gifts, enlarge my territory and broaden my horizon.
- Let me be profitable to you with my gifts.
- Help me to use my gifts to draw people to you.
- Let my gift inspire many to draw out their own gifting.
- Let your gifts in me bring upliftment and blessings to my life.
- Let my gifting bless many lives.
- Let individuals profit from my gifts, and let the body of Christ be blessed by them.
- Let me fulfil every purpose you had in mind in giving me the gifts.
- Lord, help me to stir up every gift and to be stirred up for you.

DAY THIRTY SIX

MEDITATION

Thou shalt also be a crown of glory in the hand of the LORD, and a royal diadem in the hand of thy God.

Isaiah 62:3 KJV

My confession

I am crowned by the Lord with virtue and honour.
No shame in my life.
The beauty of God is revealed in me.
By reason of his crown of honour, I am honoured by all.

Crown me, Lord

- To the Lord alone belongs the crown of glory, majesty, power, sovereignty, honour, and excellence forever.

- The Lord could crown any man or woman that pleases him with a crown of glory as it belongs to him.

- I therefore pray, Lord, according to your word above, crown me with your crown of glory.

- As Queen Esther was favoured and crowned in the midst of many women, let the crown of your glory upon me attract favour to my life.

- A crown signifies rulership and dominion. Lord, let me rule over anything that is against your purpose in my life.

- Lord, let me have dominion over the flesh and every sin that easily besets.

- The crown of Queen Vashti was removed due to the sin of pride; let pride not rule in my heart.

- Let my life be crowned with your honour, prosperity, and blessing.

- Let me be a royal diadem in your hand.

- Let me be a precious vessel fit for the master's use.

- Let me be a gem of inestimable value in your hands.

- Let your beauty shine forth and radiate through my life as you crown me.

- As a crown also signifies honour, Lord, let your honour never depart from my life.

DAY THIRTY SEVEN

MEDITATION

If they obey and serve him, they shall spend their days in prosperity, and their years in pleasures.

Job 36:11 KJV

My confession

I will continue to serve the Lord,
with all that is within me,
with all that I have.
I will serve him with the whole of my being.
Such a little sacrifice to give
for the one who gave me his all.

Reward of service

- Lord, I bless you that you are interested in rewarding diligent service.

- I bless you that you will not allow me to serve you in vain.

- I appreciate you because you recognize my service, and you will not leave me without reward.

- You have said that you are my exceeding great reward. I accept your promise into my life.

- You also promised that if I obey and serve you, I will spend my days in prosperity and my years in pleasure.

- I recognize that your promise is yea and amen, and it will be so in my life as you have promised.

- I declare that I will spend my days in prosperity.

- I declare that I will spend my years in pleasure.

- I declare that my diligent service will attract heaven's attention.

- I declare that my obedience will bring great gain into my life.

- I declare that my service to God will lead to eternal harvest and fruitfulness in my life.

- I declare that my posterity will reap the reward of my obedience and service to God.

DAY THIRTY EIGHT

MEDITATION

I will praise thee; for I am fearfully and wonderfully made: marvellous are thy works; and that my soul knoweth right well.

Psalm 139:14 KJV

My confession

I was made with care and fashioned in excellence.
I am a wonder to many.
I am the epitome of his master class.
Revealing the beauty of his creation, he has made me beautiful, and he calls me good.

Designed for purpose

- Lord, I thank you for creating me after your likeness.
- I thank you that that I was specially designed and carefully framed.
- I appreciate you for making me a total and complete being.
- I am grateful to you that I have soundness of mind, clarity of vision, and wholeness of body.
- You formed me for a purpose, and I will live a purposeful life.
- You created me fearfully and wonderfully so that your glory can be revealed in me.
- I declare that your glory is manifest in my life.
- I declare that I am God's handiwork to show forth his praise on the earth.
- I declare that I am loaded and full with God's glory and power.
- My life will proclaim his wondrous work.
- My life will shine forth and exemplify his praise.
- My hand will do the work of God.
- My heart will love God and rest in hope.
- My legs will walk in the path of truth and life.
- With the whole of my being, I will praise and exalt the Lord.

DAY THIRTY NINE

MEDITATION

Rooted and built up in him, and established in the faith, as ye have been taught, abounding therein with thanksgiving.

Colossians 2:7 KJV

My confession

I am thankful for God's love, blessings, mercies, provision, and gift.
I am thankful to be alive and well.
I am thankful to be relevant for his purpose.
I am thankful for the eyes that see, the legs that walk, and the hand that I can lift up to praise him.
I am thankful to be chosen as his child.
I am thankful that I am ever in his thoughts.

Thanksgiving

- What can I render to my God?

- He has saved me, established me, and planted me on a solid foundation.

- He has put a joy in my heart and a song in my mouth.

- He has called me his very own.

- He satisfies my need and clothes me with his mercies and tender love.

- He satisfies my mouth with good things, and my youth is daily renewed like the eagles.

- He cleanses me from sin and does not deal with me after my transgressions.

- He enfolds me in his arms and guides my feet from falling.

- He protects me from dangers and builds his edges of fire around my life.

- Therefore, my heart rejoices and my soul praises his name.

- I offer my thanksgiving and praise and declare the awesomeness of my God.

- I thank you for all you are to me and declare that you reign supreme in my life.

- I offer my thanksgiving and appreciation and declare that you are my God forever, and I will worship you all my days.

DAY FORTY

MEDITATION

But none of these things move me, neither count I my life dear unto myself, so that I might finish my course with joy, and the ministry, which I have received of the Lord Jesus, to testify the gospel of the grace of God.

Acts 20:24 KJV

My confession

I have started, and I will finish.
I will not just finish, but I will finish well.
I will accomplish my task in life.
I will fulfil purpose and destiny in this life.
I will be a worthy ambassador of his assignment and complete the work of the kingdom and life with precision and accuracy.

I will finish well

- I have set my feet on the path of this life, and I will finish my course.

- I recognize that the race is not to the swift; neither is the battle to the strong.

- Therefore, my race in life will be with the strength of God, and I will be victorious in the battles of life.

- The Lord Jesus began his ministry well, and he finished well. Therefore, I will also finish well.

- Apostle Paul was assigned to take the gospel to the Gentiles, and he finished his assignment well. I will also finish my assignment well.

- Every assignment I have been designed and purposed for in this life will be executed and completed well.

- I will not run the race of life aimlessly.

- I will not fall by the wayside.

- I will not be distracted from the mission I have been called to accomplish.

- I have been equipped to achieve success in the work of God and service of humanity in this life, and I will not fail.

- The journey is long, but the Lord will strengthen me every step of the way.

- My feet will not depart from the house of God.

- My hands will do the work of God.

- My heart will think upon those things that are true, honest, pure, lovely, and of good report as these delight the Father's heart.

- I am set to finish well and to receive the crown of righteousness that the Lord has reserved for the faithful.

YOUR INVITATION

You are invited to be among those God is calling to enter his rest and receive salvation. In John 3:16 KJV, the Bible says, 'For God so loved the world, that he gave his only begotten Son, that whosoever believeth in him should not perish, but have everlasting life.'

God loves you, and he does not want you to perish but rather to acknowledge your sin and accept the Lord Jesus Christ into your life as your Lord and Saviour, and you shall be saved. If you believe with your heart, you need to confess it with your mouth and declare the new life you now have in Jesus.

If you have decided to accept this invitation, you need to make this confession:

> Lord Jesus, I come to you as I am, a sinner in need of a saviour. I believe that you came to the world to die for my sins and on the third day you rose from the grave, thereby conquering sin and death. I now repent of my sins and submit my life to you to be my Lord and saviour, and I know that I am now saved.

Once you have made this confession, I congratulate you and welcome you to the family of God. You now have to daily read your Bible and pray to God so that you can grow spiritually. You also need to find a Bible-believing church where you can flourish through Christian fellowship and service.

++

If you gave your life to Jesus as a result of using this book and making the above salvation confession, I will love to hear from you.

Your experience
I believe this prayer book has blessed you, and if you are happy to share your experience with me, I will love to hear from you, and if you have any questions, I will love to respond to you from biblical perspective. If you also want me to join you in prayers over any specific issue(s), you can send me an email at *rr.inspiration@yahoo.co.uk*.

++

Other work by the author to be published soon:

My Quest for His Truth

Index

A

Abraham 35, 68, 71
abundance 33, 69, 75, 79, 81
Acts 20:24 96
affliction 61, 83, 85
Aigbogun, Pastor Victor 9
angels 55
atheists 11

B

Bible 83, 99
blessings 19, 30, 65
boat 79

C

charity 77
Colossians 2:7 94
crown of glory 88-9
Cyrus 18

D

deliverance 12, 15, 23, 25, 33, 49, 79
Deuteronomy:
  2:2-3 32
  2:7 36
  33:26 28
  33:7 26
diligence 7, 69, 76
divination 55

E

Ebenezer 24
Ephesians 1:3 64
evil one 48, 54-5, 57, 61, 75

F

faith 47, 61, 63, 65, 71, 77, 94
famine 68-9
fasting 12, 15-16
1 Samuel: 7:12 24
forbidden fruit 41
fountain of living water 81

G

gathering 52, 54-5
Genesis:
  26:1 68
  26:12 68
  26:13 70
  26:22 72
  38:29 74
  49 39
  49:28 38
Gentiles 97
gifting 19, 51, 83, 87
God 18, 20, 22-3, 31, 51
grace 19, 23, 53, 60-1, 75, 87
green pastures 80-1

H

harvest 69, 77, 91
healing 12, 15, 23, 27, 46
heaven 29, 31, 39
Holy Spirit 45, 51, 57, 76

I

iniquity 35, 46-7, 75
invitation 98-9
Isaac 68, 71
Isaiah:
  6:7 46

101

45:1-3 18
54:13 50
54:14 52
54:15 54
54:17 56
62:3 88
Israelites 31, 33, 37

J

Jeremiah 17:7 42
Jesus 15-16, 29, 31, 33, 41, 49, 53, 56, 64, 71, 75-6, 79, 99-100
Job:
  22:21 34
  36:11 90
John 3:16 99

K

kindness 76-7
kingdom of darkness 55
knowledge 51, 66-7, 76-7

L

Lord Jesus
  Resurrection 99
Lord's Prayer 15
loving-kindness 59

M

manna 31
Mark 6:48 78
Matthew 4:19 62
ministry 15, 55, 67, 71, 96-7

N

Nehemiah 2:18 20
Numbers 14:28 16

O

obedience 91
oppression 39, 52-3

P

Paul (apostle) 97
peace 21, 34-5, 50-1, 72, 77-9
poverty 49, 59, 75, 79
prayer communion 11, 15
prayer life 9, 11, 71
prayers
  ineffective 9
pride 89
promised land 32-3, 41
promises 9, 20-1, 33, 91
prosperity 21, 23, 31, 33, 69, 72, 75, 79, 81, 89-91
Proverbs 2:6-7 66
Psalms:
  23:1 80
  23:6 44
  37:4 40
  84:11 60
  102:24 82
  139:14 92
  143:8 58
  144:12 84

Q

Queen Esther 89
Queen Vashti 89

R

reward 91
righteousness 30-1, 56, 97
rolling stone 32
royal diadem 88-9

S

salvation 23
Samuel 21, 24
2 Corinthians:
  1:10 48
  9:10-11 30
2 Peter 1:5-8 76
2 Timothy 1:6 86
servitude 75
shepherd 80-1
sin 41, 47, 61, 75, 89, 95, 99
Solomon (king) 67

U

universe 62

V

victory 23, 25, 33, 55-6, 79

W

weapon of destruction 56-7
wisdom 18-19, 23, 50-1, 59, 66-7